DO-IT-YOURSELF PODCAST LAUNCH

WORKBOOK

THIS WORKBOOK BELONGS TO:

_____

Welcome to the Branded Family!

Hi! We're Larry Roberts and Sara Lohse, the hosts of the Branded podcasts and professional podcast producers and coaches.

Podcasting is an innovative medium that enables you to share your voice, stories, insights, or expertise with the world. We created this quick-start guide to help you get your own show ready and launched in just four weeks.

Take the time to read through each section, do the exercises, and fill the open pages with notes and thoughts to guide you through the process.

If you need any help along the way, we offer one-time and ongoing coaching to answer questions, develop creative strategies, or offer feedback on your progress.

Reach out to us at hello@listentobranded.com for more information on coaching packages and pricing.

Happy podcasting!

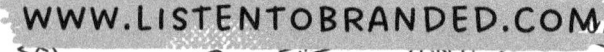

Getting Started

Embarking on your podcasting journey can be an exhilarating experience, but it's also one that requires careful planning and preparation. To help streamline the process and set you up for success, we've curated a comprehensive Podcast Launch Checklist that sorts all the necessary tasks into four weeks. This step-by-step guide is designed to walk you through every crucial stage in your podcast development, from conceptualization to your ultimate launch.

Our checklist covers all the essentials: picking a unique podcast name, researching its availability, and securing a corresponding URL. It will guide you through the creative process of designing eye-catching cover art and crafting an engaging show description.

You'll find guidance on structuring your show for consistency, selecting the right Apple Podcast categories for optimal visibility, and creating a wishlist of guests. We also cover the practical aspects of setting a sustainable recording schedule and, finally, scheduling your big launch date. With this checklist, you'll be well-equipped to navigate the podcasting landscape and ready to make your mark in the world of audio content.

WEEK ONE

PLANNING

TO DO LIST

- ⃝ PICK A PODCAST NAME
- ⃝ RESEARCH NAME AVAILABILITY
- ⃝ MAKE A LIST OF RELEVANT KEYWORDS
- ⃝ BUY RELEVANT URL
- ⃝ RESEARCH SIMILAR SHOWS
- ⃝ IDENTIFY UNIQUE LISTENING PROPOSITION
- ⃝ DETERMINE YOUR TARGET AUDIENCE
- ⃝ DESIGN COVER ART
- ⃝ WRITE SHOW DESCRIPTION
- ⃝ DETERMINE SHOW STRUCTURE
- ⃝ DETERMINE APPLE PODCAST CATEGORIES
- ⃝ MAKE GUEST WISHLIST
- ⃝ SET A RECORDING SCHEDULE
- ⃝ SCHEDULE LAUNCH DATE

Pick a Podcast Name

Choosing a podcast name is a crucial step in your planning process. Your podcast name is the first impression potential listeners have of your show, so it should be engaging, descriptive, and memorable. It should ideally communicate the essence of your content, spark curiosity, and resonate with your target audience. You may want to incorporate keywords related to your podcast's theme to enhance visibility in search results.

While you want your name to be cute and memorable, you also want it to be easily found when someone is looking for shows on your topic.

Research Name Availability

Researching name availability is a vital step in establishing your podcast. This process ensures your chosen name isn't already taken, reducing potential confusion and maintaining your podcast's unique identity. Start by checking major podcast directories like Apple Podcasts, Spotify, and Google Podcasts to see if your potential name is already in use.

Additionally, perform a general internet search to detect any lesser-known podcasts or other entities using your proposed name. Also, check domain availability if you plan to create a website for your podcast. Consider using tools like GoDaddy's Domain Name Search or Namecheap. Remember, the goal is to secure a unique name that listeners can easily associate with your content. It's also a good idea to verify the name isn't trademarked to avoid legal complications. Websites like the U.S. Patent and Trademark Office (USPTO) can help with this.

Research Relevant Keywords

Keywords are how all types of content get found online, including podcasts. If someone is searching for a podcast about money, having the keyword "money" in your title and description will help your show get found.

You can use tools like the Google Keyword Planner to find out how popular different keywords are and get suggestions for similar keywords that will help you get found.

When you start writing your title and description, you'll want to include as many keywords as you can.

Buy Relevant URL

Once you've selected a unique podcast name and verified its availability, the next step is to purchase a relevant URL, or domain name. This URL typically serves as the address for your podcast's website, offering a central hub where listeners can learn more about your show, access episodes, and contact you.

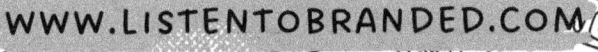

SEO for Podcasts

Besides word-of-mouth, Search Engine Optimization (SEO) is the most important thing your podcast needs to be found.

Without getting too in the weeds of SEO, the basic concept you'll want to understand is **keywords.**

Keywords are the terms that people search on Google when they're looking for something like a podcast. We talked about these in Week 1 when we were planning our show's concept.

Good keywords should be in your **titles**, **show notes**, and **descriptions** so listeners interested in your topic can find your show.

We always recommend transcribing each episode and adding the transcript to the episode's page on your website. This will make sure each keyword that is spoken on your show is accounted for in the episode's SEO.

Having links on your podcast's website also boosts the SEO, which is one of the reasons we always recommend including links to your guests' websites in the show notes.

If your podcast is on YouTube, you can add timestamps to the descriptions for when you talk about specific keywords or topics, which will also help viewers find your show.

DETAILS

TITLE IDEAS

AVAILABLE URLS

KEYWORDS

Research Similar Shows

Knowing who else is creating content on your topic can be helpful for many reasons. For one, it can show you if there are any niches within your topic that are not yet being covered so you can fill that gap. Secondly, you can start building a relationship with those hosts in order to help promote each other later.

Podcasters are generally collaborative and happy to work with other creators, just ask nicely and lead with relationship-building rather than a sales pitch.

Determine Your Unique Listening Proposition

You just did the research to find out what other podcasts are talking about within your topic. What makes yours unique? Why would a listener choose your show over another?

This could be your niche, your background, your format, or any other detail that makes your show stand out in a positive way. You'll want to communicate these points when you write your show description.

Determine Your Target Audience

You're creating a podcast, but who are you creating it for? Knowing who your target audience is will guide the content you create, help you craft your calls to action, and determine which online platforms you should be promoting on.

DETAILS

SIMILAR SHOWS

UNIQUE LISTENING PROPOSITIONS

TARGET AUDIENCE

Design Cover Art

Designing cover art is an important step in establishing your podcast's brand. The cover art is the visual representation of your podcast and often the first thing potential listeners see when browsing podcast directories. A compelling, professional-looking cover art can significantly impact your podcast's attractiveness and potentially increase your listenership.

Your cover art should ideally reflect the tone, content, and personality of your podcast. It should be visually appealing, and the title should be easy to read even when the image is small, as it often appears as a thumbnail on podcast platforms. Use colors and fonts that are consistent with your brand and that stand out.

You can design your cover art using various tools, from professional software like Adobe Photoshop or Illustrator to free online tools like Canva, which offers numerous templates. Alternatively, you can hire a graphic designer. Ensure that your design meets the specifications of podcast platforms, typically a square image in high resolution (for example, Apple Podcasts recommends a size of 3000x3000 pixels in JPEG or PNG format). Keep in mind copyright laws and use only images and designs you have rights to use.

PRO TIP: A LOT OF PEOPLE WANT TO PUT THEIR PHOTO ON THEIR COVER, BUT UNLESS YOUR FACE IS WIDELY RECOGNIZED, THERE ARE BETTER WAYS TO FILL THE SPACE.

COVER ART INSPO

SHOWS WITH ART I LOVE

IDEA DOODLES

show name

hosted by

Write Show Description

Crafting a compelling show description is an essential part of setting up your podcast. Your show description, also known as a podcast summary or blurb, provides potential listeners with insight into what your podcast is about. It's an opportunity to hook your audience, convey the value of your show, and encourage them to hit 'play.'

Begin with a powerful and concise introduction that encapsulates the essence of your podcast. Explain who the podcast is for, the topics or themes you'll cover, and what listeners can expect to gain from your show. Are you providing advice, sharing stories, sparking debates, or offering a unique perspective on a particular subject? Make sure this is clear in your description.

Don't forget to showcase your podcast's personality in your description. If your podcast is humorous, let that show in your wording. If it's a serious deep dive into complex topics, maintain a professional and authoritative tone.

It's worth noting that Apple Podcasts, one of the most widely used podcast directories, allows up to 4000 characters in a podcast description. This space affords you the opportunity to dive deeper into the aspects that make your podcast unique. While the length of your description can vary, it's essential to use this space effectively.

Consider detailing any regular segments, the frequency of episodes, or share a glimpse of what's coming in the first few episodes.

Ultimately, your podcast description should not only attract potential listeners but also set the correct expectations for what your podcast will deliver. With the right blend of information and allure, your description can become a powerful tool in converting casual browsers into loyal listeners.

You'll want to incorporate your keywords, too, for added discoverability!

Show Description Formula

Here is a simple formula to get you started on your description. Once you have this outline, you can make it your own and add your personality!

Welcome to _____,

(PODCAST NAME)

the podcast that _____

(PURPOSE OF THE SHOW)

for _____.

(TARGET AUDIENCE)

I'm your host _____ and on this

(YOUR NAME)

podcast, you will gain _____

(UNIQUE LISTENING PROP)

as we dive into conversations around

_____.

(KEYWORDS)

DESCRIPTION DRAFT

Determine Show Structure

Determining your show structure is a critical part of podcast planning. The structure provides a consistent format for your podcast, which can help keep your content organized and easy for listeners to follow. Some common elements you might include are an introduction, main content, and closing remarks.

The introduction typically includes a welcome message, an overview of the episode's content, and often a brief mention of the podcast's sponsor.

The main content varies depending on your podcast's theme, and it could be an interview, a monologue, a discussion, storytelling, or a combination.

The closing remarks might include a summary, a call to action (such as asking listeners to subscribe, review, or visit your website), and a teaser for the next episode. Remember, consistency is key in a show structure, but there's room for flexibility.

Tailor your structure to best suit your content and audience.

Determine Apple Podcast Categories

Choosing the correct Apple Podcast category for your show is more than just an organizational step; it's a strategic decision that can significantly impact your podcast's visibility and success. The category you choose determines where your podcast will appear within the Apple Podcasts directory, making it easier for potential listeners interested in your subject matter to discover your show.

By aligning your podcast with the right category, you connect with a targeted audience who are already seeking the type of content you provide. This can lead to increased listenership, higher engagement, and stronger loyalty among your listeners. Moreover, by standing out in a specific category, your podcast can gain more traction and possibly chart in that category, offering further exposure. So, don't underestimate the power of picking the correct Apple Podcast category—it's a key factor in positioning your podcast for success.

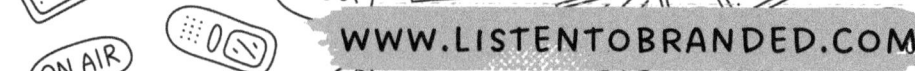

APPLE PODCAST CATEGORIES

○ ARTS
  ○ BOOKS
  ○ DESIGN
  ○ FASHION & BEAUTY
  ○ FOOD
  ○ PERFORMING ARTS
  ○ VISUAL ARTS

○ COMEDY
  ○ COMEDY INTERVIEWS
  ○ IMPROV
  ○ STAND-UP

○ BUSINESS
  ○ CAREERS
  ○ ENTREPRENEURSHIP
  ○ INVESTING
  ○ MANAGEMENT
  ○ MARKETING
  ○ NON-PROFIT

○ EDUCATION
  ○ COURSES
  ○ HOW TO
  ○ LANGUAGE LEARNING
  ○ SELF-IMPROVEMENT

○ FICTION
  ○ COMEDY FICTION
  ○ DRAMA
  ○ SCIENCE FICTION

○ GOVERNMENT

○ HISTORY

PRO TIP:
STUCK BETWEEN A FEW CATEGORIES? RESEARCH HOW MANY SHOWS ARE IN EACH TO SEE WHERE THERE'S LESS COMPETITION

HEALTH&FITNESS
- ○ ALTERNATIVE HEALTH
- ○ FITNESS
- ○ MEDICINE
- ○ MENTAL HEALTH
- ○ NUTRITION
- ○ SEXUALITY

LEISURE
- ○ ANIMATION & MANGA
- ○ AUTOMOTIVE
- ○ AVIATION
- ○ CRAFTS
- ○ GAMES
- ○ HOBBIES
- ○ HOME & GARDEN
- ○ VIDEO GAMES

NEWS
- ○ BUSINESS NEWS
- ○ DAILY NEWS
- ○ ENTERTAINMENT NEWS
- ○ NEWS COMMENTARY
- ○ POLITICS
- ○ SPORTS NEWS
- ○ TECH NEWS

KIDS&FAMILY
- ○ EDUCATION FOR KIDS
- ○ PARENTING
- ○ PETS & ANIMALS
- ○ STORIES FOR KIDS

MUSIC
- ○ MUSIC COMMENTARY
- ○ MUSIC HISTORY
- ○ MUSIC INTERVIEWS

RELIGION&SPIRITUALITY
- ○ BUDDHISM
- ○ CHRISTIANITY
- ○ HINDUISM
- ○ ISLAM
- ○ JUDAISM
- ○ RELIGION
- ○ SPIRITUALITY

SCIENCE

- ASTRONOMY
- CHEMISTRY
- EARTH SCIENCES
- LIFE SCIENCES
- MATHEMATICS
- NATURAL SCIENCES
- NATURE
- PHYSICS
- SOCIAL SCIENCES

SOCIETY & CULTURE

- DOCUMENTARY
- PERSONAL JOURNALS
- PHILOSOPHY
- PLACES & TRAVEL
- RELATIONSHIPS

SPORTS

- BASEBALL
- BASKETBALL
- CRICKET
- FANTASY SPORTS
- FOOTBALL
- GOLF
- HOCKEY
- RUGBY
- SOCCER
- SWIMMING
- TENNIS
- VOLLEYBALL
- WILDERNESS
- WRESTLING

TECHNOLOGY

TRUE CRIME

TV & FILM

- AFTER SHOWS
- FILM HISTORY
- FILM INTERVIEWS
- FILM REVIEWS
- TV REVIEWS

Make a Guest Wishlist

Bringing guests on your show can help to broaden your appeal, attract new listeners, and boost your credibility within your podcast's topic or industry. Make a wishlist of individuals whose expertise, experiences, or perspectives align with your podcast's theme and would provide value to your listeners.

This wishlist can even serve as a motivating goal and a measure of your podcast's growth. Landing a guest from your wishlist can be an exciting achievement, marking a milestone in your podcasting journey. It's a tangible indication that your show is attracting attention and gaining influence within your chosen field. Plus, a high-profile guest can potentially open doors to other noteworthy guests, helping to perpetuate your podcast's growth and success.

Remember, guests who are well known and have large followings can be great, but make sure they are bringing more value than just their names.

Even guests who aren't well known but have great stories can bring in download numbers. Be picky with who you allow on your show. At the end of the day, your goal is always to create great content.

Having guests who also host podcasts can help ensure the audio quality stays high.

PRO TIP:
TRADING GUEST SPOTS ON YOUR PODCAST FOR GUEST SPOTS ON SIMILAR PODCASTS CAN BE A FAST WAY TO GROW YOUR AUDIENCE.

GUEST WISHLIST

NAME & TOPIC	INVITED	RECORDED
Larry and Sara	◯	◯
	◯	◯
	◯	◯
	◯	◯
	◯	◯
	◯	◯
	◯	◯
	◯	◯
	◯	◯
	◯	◯
	◯	◯
	◯	◯
	◯	◯
	◯	◯
	◯	◯

Set a Recording Schedule

Establishing a consistent recording schedule is an integral part of running a successful podcast. Your recording schedule ensures you have a regular stream of content and helps maintain your listeners' interest. It also allows you to plan your time efficiently and meet your podcasting commitments alongside other personal or professional obligations.

The frequency of your podcast episodes depends on your available time, content, and listener expectations. You could choose to release new episodes daily, weekly, bi-weekly, or monthly.

Keep in mind that consistency is key, as regular uploads can help build listener loyalty. When scheduling your recording times, consider the time it takes for preparation, recording, editing, and promoting each episode.

Remember, it's better to start with a less frequent schedule and increase over time than to start with an unsustainable pace. Be sure to communicate your publishing schedule to your listeners, so they know when to expect new episodes.

RECORDING SCHEDULE

1. I WILL RECORD EPISODES _____ TIMES PER MONTH.
2. I WILL RECORD ON _____. (THE FIRST MONDAY, EVERY FRIDAY, ETC.)
3. I WILL RELEASE EPISODES _____. (WEEKLY, MONTHLY, ETC.)

EPISODE # AND TITLE	RECORDING DATE	RELEASE DATE

Schedule a Launch Date

Scheduling a launch date for your podcast is a significant step in your planning process. A launch date is the day your podcast goes live and becomes available to the public. Having a set launch date helps you create a timeline for all the necessary tasks leading up to the big day, such as recording, editing, setting up your podcast host, submitting your podcast to directories, and promoting the launch.

When choosing a launch date, consider your production timeline. Ensure you have ample time to produce high-quality episodes and troubleshoot any issues that might arise. Many podcasters opt to have several episodes ready before the launch, so listeners can dive deeper if they enjoy the first episode. This can also alleviate the pressure of immediate content creation post-launch.

Take into account the promotional activities you'll need to carry out before the launch. You might want to build anticipation through social media, your website, or an email newsletter. A good rule of thumb is to start promoting 2-4 weeks before the launch.

Lastly, remember to choose a launch date and day that suits your target audience's listening habits. Once you've selected a launch date, stick to it and build your pre-launch activities around it.

I WILL LAUNCH MY PODCAST ON

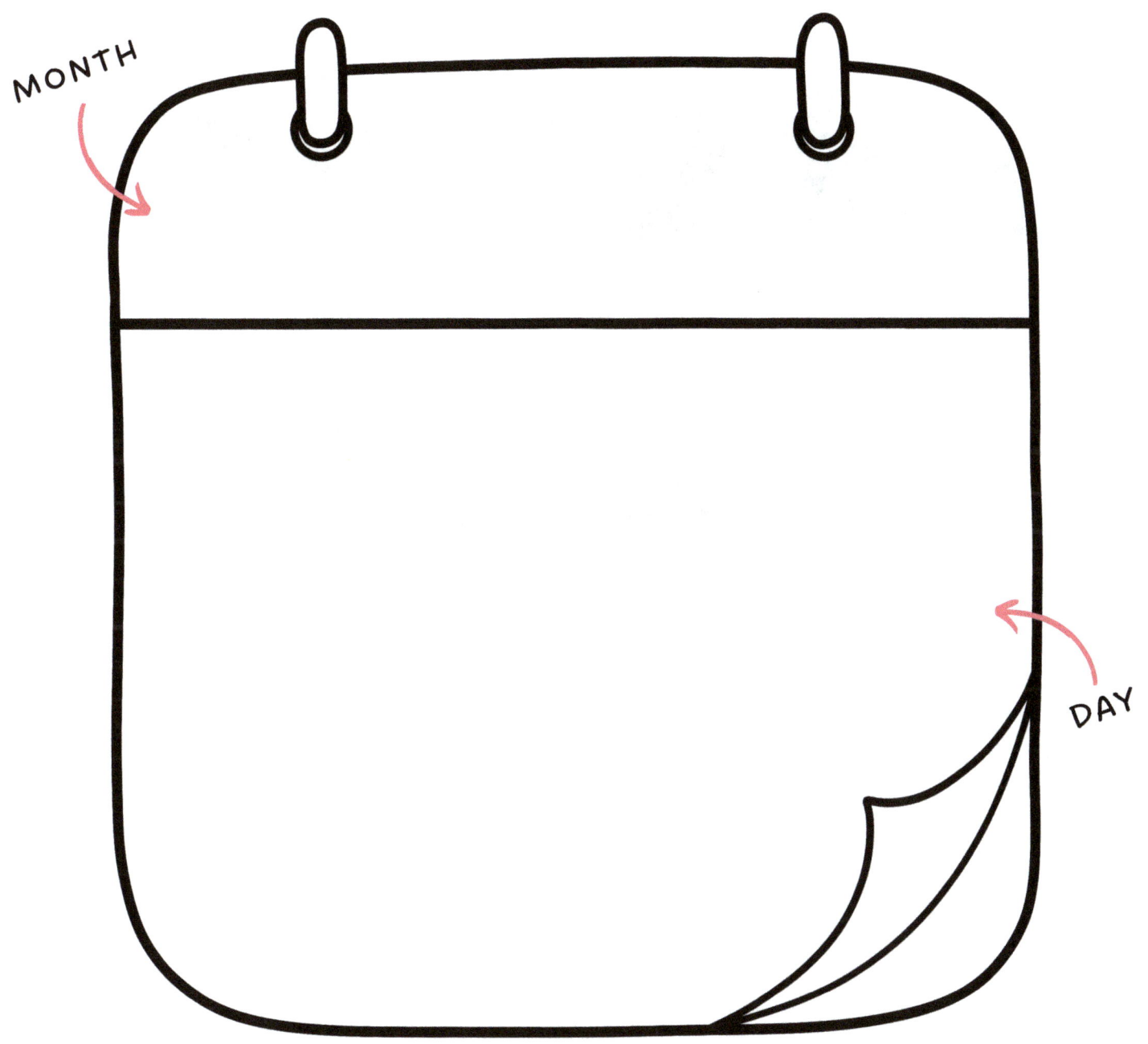

MONTH

DAY

WEEK TWO

TECH

TO DO LIST

- ⭕ PURCHASE EQUIPMENT
- ⭕ SET UP RECORDING STUDIO
- ⭕ SET UP STUDIO LIGHTING
- ⭕ CHOOSE HOSTING PLATFORM
- ⭕ TEST MIC, HEADPHONES, AND CAMERA
- ⭕ CREATE A WEBSITE
- ⭕
- ⭕
- ⭕
- ⭕
- ⭕
- ⭕
- ⭕
- ⭕

Purchasing Podcast Equipment

Embarking on your podcast journey doesn't have to break the bank, nor does it mean you should compromise on the quality of your content. Our Introductory Podcast Equipment Package has been carefully curated with the budget-conscious podcaster in mind, ensuring you get the best bang for your buck without sacrificing audio excellence.

We understand that starting a podcast can feel overwhelming, especially when it comes to technical aspects like equipment. That's why this package is designed to be as straightforward as possible. It includes a high-quality yet affordable microphone that delivers crisp, clear audio, a pair of comfortable headphones for precise sound monitoring, and an easy-to-use audio interface for seamless recording and editing.

This package is more than just a collection of equipment; it's your entry ticket into the world of podcasting. By balancing affordability with quality, we've ensured that you can focus on what truly matters: creating engaging content that resonates with your audience.

EQUIPMENT

LOGITECH STREAMCAM

PLUG-AND-PLAY WEBCAM
FOR HD VIDEO

FOCUSRITE VOCASTER 1

PODCASTING INTERFACE
FOR THE SOLO CREATOR

RODE PODMIC

PODCASTING MICROPHONE
FOR PROFESSIONAL SOUND
QUALITY

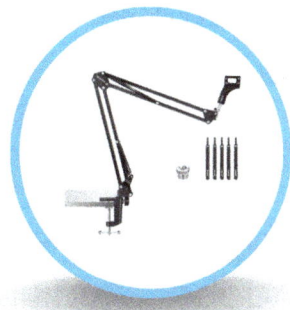

MIC BOOM ARM

MICROPHONE ARM TO
MAXIMIZE DESK SPACE

AUDIO-TECHNICA ATH-M20X

STUDIO-QUALITY
HEADPHONES

WWW.LISTENTOBRANDED.COM

Setting Up a Recording Studio

Setting up a recording studio—whether in person or virtual—is an important step to getting started.

For In-Person Recordings:

First, select a quiet room with minimal noise and echo. Soft furnishings like carpets and curtains can help absorb sound. Next, prepare the space by removing or turning off any noisy appliances or devices and notifying others in your household of your recording schedule to minimize interruptions.

Once the space is prepared, set up your equipment. A dynamic microphone is a good choice for home studios as it picks up less background noise. Place the microphone on a stand and use a pop filter to reduce plosive sounds. Use closed-back headphones to monitor your recording without any sound leakage. Connect your microphone to your computer via an audio interface, which converts the analog signal from your microphone into a digital signal your computer can use. If you have multiple microphones or other audio sources, a mixer can help control the audio levels.

Next, install and configure your chosen recording software on your computer. Popular choices include Adobe Audition, Audacity (free), and GarageBand (for Mac). Do a test recording to check the sound quality and make any necessary adjustments to your setup or recording levels. Finally, start recording your podcast, making sure to monitor the audio levels throughout.

Setting Up a Recording Studio

For Virtual/Remote Recordings:

Setting up a home-based podcast recording studio for virtual or remote recordings involves similar steps to in-person recording, with a few key differences. First, select a quiet room with minimal noise and echo. Prepare your equipment as described for in-person recording, including setting up your microphone, headphones, and audio interface.

Next, choose recording software that allows for remote recording. Examples include Streamyard, Riverside and SquadCast. Set up your internet connection, ensuring it is stable and fast. A wired connection is preferred, and close any unnecessary applications that may use bandwidth.

Coordinate with your guest to ensure they also have a good quality microphone and headphones, and a stable internet connection. Send them the link to join the remote recording session. Do a test recording with your guest to check the audio quality and make any necessary adjustments. Start recording your podcast, making sure to monitor the audio levels throughout.

In both scenarios, remember to save your recordings in a quality lossless format like .WAV for the best audio quality. After recording, you can edit your podcast using audio editing software and then export it in a compressed format like .MP3 for distribution.

Setting Up Your Hosting

Your podcast host is simply the platform that you upload your podcast to. Basically, it's the podcast's home.

When you set up your hosting, you will be able to connect the platform to the different podcast players (like Apple Podcasts, Spotify, and iHeart) so that all you do each time you upload an episode is add it to the hosting platform. The platform itself will disseminate the episode to each of the players via RSS feed.

There are tons of different options for podcast hosts to choose from. Some good ones we've used are **Blubrry, Captivate.fm, Megaphone, and LibSyn.**

While their basic purposes are the same, every hosting platform is different.

When you're choosing one, look at the cost, the analytics they provide, how user-friendly they are, and any other factor that is important to you.

Because our show is hosted in Blubrry, you can get your first month free if you our promo code **Branded** when you sign up.

Creating a Website

Every podcast should have a website so you have one consistent place to send your listeners that is accessible (meaning not Apple podcasts since some people have Android).

If you currently have a website for a personal or professional brand that your show is connected to, you can add the podcast to the existing site as its own page. Each episode should also have its own page, set up basically the way you'd set up a blog post.

If you do it this way, we still recommend buying a URL unique to the podcast and having it forward directly to the podcast's landing page.

If you don't currently have a website and don't dabble in development or programming, there are user-friendly tools available.

Our favorite that we use for the Branded podcast and our clients is **PodPage**.

PodPage lets you connect your show's RSS feed and then creates a basic website for you, with customization options once it's set up. The reason this is a cool tool is that the site will automatically pull your new episodes and create pages for each, plus it will pull reviews from Apple Podcasts and let your guests fill out their intake forms right on the site.

You can use our code Branded when you sign up here, too!

WEEK THREE

CREATION

TO DO LIST

- ⭕ BUILD A CALL TO ACTION (CTA)
- ⭕ RECORD YOUR TRAILER
- ⭕ RECORD YOUR FIRST 3-5 EPISODES
- ⭕ CREATE YOUR SHOW NOTES
- ⭕
- ⭕
- ⭕
- ⭕
- ⭕
- ⭕
- ⭕
- ⭕
- ⭕

Creating Your Call-To-Action

Every podcast and each of its episodes should have a call-to-action, or CTA.

This is the action you want your audience to take after they listen to your show. Common CTAs include:

- Subscribe to the show
- Leave a review
- Share the show with your friends
- Send us feedback

You want to be careful to only include one CTA each time so you don't overwhelm the listener with too many things to do.

If you're using the podcast for business purposes, that CTA may be to download a lead magnet so you can get their information and market your products and services to them.

If you want to learn more about lead magnets, Sara has a free e-book all about them that you can download at www.favoriteleadmagnets.com.

See what we did there? That's a lead magnet lead magnet!

Recording a Podcast Trailer

A podcast trailer serves as an exciting preview of your show, offering potential listeners a taste of what to expect. The trailer introduces your show's theme, style, host(s), and potential topics, providing a snapshot of your podcast that can captivate listeners and persuade them to subscribe. You can use your podcast description as a start, and ad-lib as you record to make it more natural and conversational.

One major advantage of a podcast trailer is its shareability. Trailers are typically short—often between one to three minutes long—making them easy to share across various platforms, such as social media, email newsletters, and on your podcast website. This creates buzz around your show before its official launch, helping to build an initial audience.

On the technical side, in order to establish an RSS feed for your podcast, you need to publish an episode. The trailer can serve as this episode, letting you establish your RSS, submit your show to podcast directories, increase your podcast's discoverability, and allow listeners to subscribe and receive the first episode as soon as it's released.

Recording a podcast trailer also allows you to practice and refine your recording and editing process before launching into full-length episodes. It gives you a chance to become comfortable with your equipment and software, experiment with different podcasting styles, and find your unique voice as a podcaster. Overall, a well-crafted podcast trailer can significantly enhance your podcast launch, helping to build anticipation, attract listeners, and set the tone for your show.

Scripting Your Trailer

You want to put thought into what you include in your trailer, as it will be the first taste of your show that a listener gets. Here are a few key components you'll want to include:

Introduction: Introduce the show, the hosts, who it's for, and what it will be about.

Format: Let the listener know what to expect. How often do you release episodes? Is this a solo show or will you bring on guests?

Highlights: What are you excited to bring your listeners? Do you have great guests lined up? A cool ULP? Let them know!

Call to Action: What should a person do when they listen to your trailer? Let them know where to find your show (preferably your website) and that they should subscribe!

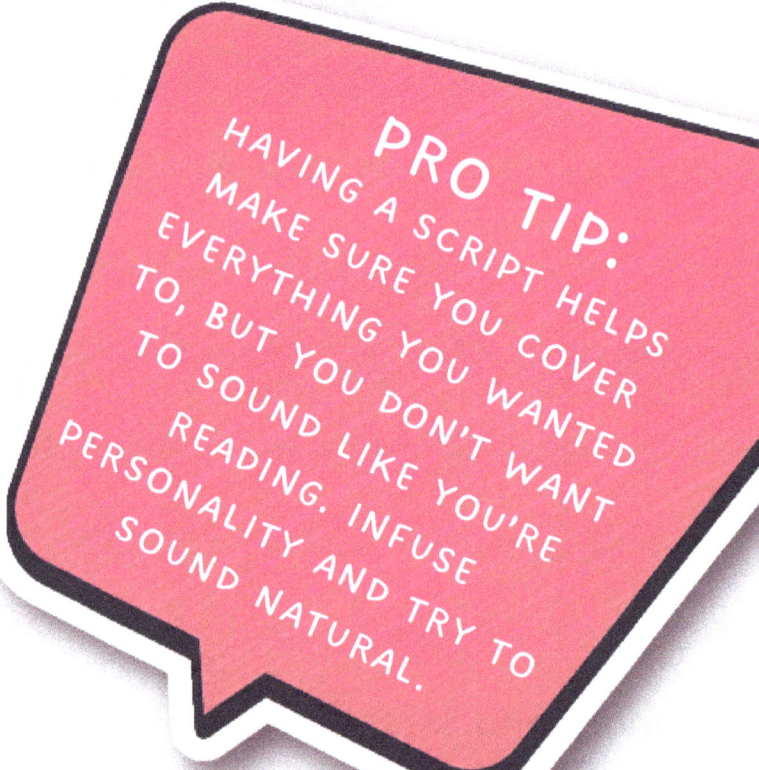

PRO TIP: HAVING A SCRIPT HELPS MAKE SURE YOU COVER EVERYTHING YOU WANTED TO, BUT YOU DON'T WANT TO SOUND LIKE YOU'RE READING. INFUSE PERSONALITY AND TRY TO SOUND NATURAL.

TRAILER SCRIPT

Best Practices for Recording Solo Episodes

Plan: For a solo podcast episode, you want to go in with a plan. Select the topic you want to cover in each episode ahead of time. While you don't want to script out what you want to say, you do want to create an outline so you stay organized and on track while recording.

Research: Recording a podcast can feel stressful at first, so don't assume you can rely on your memory completely. Especially if covering a complex topic, do your research and have notes ready so you can cite facts, statistics, and anecdotes for support.

Recording Technique: Always be speaking clearly, at a natural pace, and enunciating your words. It's okay if you fumble your words when you're recording. When this happens, stop speaking for a second and then start again at the beginning of the sentence. This will make it easy to remove the flub in editing.

Best Practices for Recording with a Guest

Preparation: Prior to the recording, research your guest's background, interests, and expertise thoroughly to form meaningful questions that will generate a compelling discussion. Share these questions with your guest in advance to help them prepare as well.

Technical Aspects: Ensure both you and your guest have reliable recording equipment and a quiet environment to minimize technical glitches and background noise. Check your internet connection if you're recording remotely and select a recording platform that's easy for both parties to use.

Time Management: Be respectful of your guest's time. Make sure to start and finish the recording as scheduled. Also, don't let the conversation drift too far off-topic, keeping it focused on your planned questions and themes.

Recording Etiquette: Make your guest feel comfortable and valued. Listen actively when they speak, maintain a friendly tone, and give them space to fully articulate their thoughts.

Clear Instructions: Provide your guest with clear instructions about the podcast process, including when they should be ready to record, what platform you'll be using, and how long the recording will last.

Post-Recording Process: After the recording, thank your guest for their time. Inform them about when the episode will be released and how you will promote it. Encourage them to share the episode with their own audience once it goes live.

Create Your Show Notes

Every podcast episode needs show notes. This is an episode-level description that will be shown by the podcast players as well as on your website.

As we've already discussed, show notes are important for adding SEO power to your show, as well as giving the listener an idea of what to expect.

Your show notes should include:

- A summary of what the episode is about,

- An introduction to your guest and links to their website and/or social media,

- Key takeaways that the listener will learn,

- Links to any additional resources mentioned,

- And a CTA.

In addition to the show notes, you should also transcribe your podcast episodes! This helps the show be accessible to the Deaf and hard of hearing, is great for SEO, and can make it easier to write blog posts later.

WEEK FOUR

LAUNCH

TO DO LIST

- ◯ CREATE A MARKETING PLAN
- ◯ PUBLISH YOUR PODCAST TRAILER
- ◯ PROMOTE TRAILER
- ◯ PUBLISH YOUR FIRST 3 EPISODES
- ◯ PROMOTE, PROMOTE, PROMOTE!
- ◯
- ◯
- ◯
- ◯
- ◯
- ◯
- ◯
- ◯
- ◯

Launching Your Podcast

The official launch of your podcast is a milestone moment that lays the foundation for the success of your show. It is the culmination of all your preparation and hard work, where everything comes together and your podcast finally becomes accessible to listeners worldwide. However, a successful launch requires a well-executed plan, which involves more than just releasing your first episode. It encompasses strategic promotion, audience engagement, and the launch of multiple episodes.

Strategic promotion is essential in the run-up to and during your podcast launch. This could involve sharing your podcast trailer, creating buzz on social media, engaging with potential listeners on relevant online platforms, or even hosting a launch event. Your goal is to build awareness and anticipation around your podcast, encouraging as many people as possible to subscribe and listen to your first episode upon release.

On your actual launch day, instead of releasing just one episode, consider releasing three to five episodes at once. This provides new listeners with a deeper dive into your content, giving them a chance to get hooked on your podcast right away. Once your podcast is live, encourage your listeners to leave reviews and share your podcast with others. These early engagements can be crucial in propelling your podcast up the ranks in podcast directories, leading to increased visibility and more listeners. Overall, launching your podcast is a multi-faceted process that, when done right, can set a strong foundation for your show's success.

Creating a Marketing Plan

Now that you're about to launch your show, how do you plan to market it?

Here are a few ideas to help you create your own marketing plan:

- When you set up your hosting, make sure you connect your show to all the major players! Even if you don't listen on a certain app, doesn't mean potential listeners don't.

- Use social media. Some people will make social media profiles specifically for their shows which can be great for branding, or you can use your personal or business pages to promote your show.

- If you have an email list already, you'll want to include email marketing in your plan. If you don't, a lead magnet is a great way to start building one.

- Repurpose your content! Each podcast episode can be promoted in countless ways if you repurpose it.

- If there are shows in the same or similar niche as yours (there will be, we can almost guarantee it), reach out to their hosts and suggest a promo swap or even to be a guest on each other's show.

Repurposing Your Content

Repurposing your content is vital to your marketing and promotion.

Each episode can be turned into countless other pieces of content, such as:

Short-form videos. Having a full episode is great, but for social media, you want to cut it up. Creating Reels, TikToks, and YouTube shorts will make your show far easier for you and your audience to share.

Blogs. You've already transcribed your show, but nobody really wants to read a transcript. Take the transcript a step further by turning it into a more reader-friendly blog. If you covered more than one topic in the episode, you can write a blog for each topic. This helps get your content in front of people who prefer reading to listening and adds greater SEO power to your website.

Graphics. There are so many different types of graphics you can make for your show. Use your guest's headshot to announce their appearance. Create quote graphics when you or a guest say something impactful. Make a few graphics that go together for a carousel post.

Audiograms. While video is currently performing the best, some podcasters may still choose to stay audio-only. If this is you, turn a graphic into an audiogram by overlaying an audio clip from your episode.

Publishing Your Podcast

On launch day, you want to publish at least three episodes so your show is instantly bingeable.

You publish your show through your podcast hosting player. A few things to remember:

1. Each episode should have its own page on your website, which should include the episode's media player, an embedded YouTube video, direct links to the episode on the biggest podcast players, show notes, the guest's profile, and the transcript.

2. Even if you're using something like PodPage to automatically add your episodes to your website, you'll still want to log in and make sure everything is appearing the way you want it to.

PodPage lets every guest have a profile, but you still need to manually link that profile to the episode.

3. Many players now allow for episodic cover art, so you're able to design cover art specific for each episode to include the guest's headshot or the title of that episode.

YOU DID IT!

Congratulations, you professional podcaster.

Now you have a podcast and your episodes are live. All you have to do now is keep going.

Promote your show everywhere, continue to create episodes and content, and ask for feedback as you go so you're able to improve along the way.

Plus, we're here to help!

The Branded team (AKA Sara and Larry) offers single-session or ongoing coaching for podcasters, as well as podcast audits to give you a thorough idea of how your podcast is doing and how you can make it better.

To find out more about working with us, you can email us at hello@listentobranded.com or fill out the contact form on our website, www.listentobranded.com.

If this book helped you create a podcast, email it to us so we can listen, review, and share it!

About the Branded Team

Larry Roberts is the founder of Red Hat Media, a company dedicated to helping business leaders embrace their brand stories, and frame their next chapters, and position themselves strongly within their industry.

He is one of the most well-known creators in podcasting and has been featured on stage and virtually at events like Podfest, Podcast Movement, Outlier Podcast Festival, and Entrepreneurs Organization.

    @thelarryroberts

🌐 www.redhatmedia.io

Sara Lohse launched Favorite Daughter Media to help mission-driven brands and creators amplify their social reach and impact.

She combines content creation with business strategy, introducing a fresh perspective and emerging media trends to new or established brands. Her tips and insights have been heard at Podfest, FinCon, PodPros Summit, and Outlier Podcast Festival.

    @favoritedaughtermedia

🌐 www.favoritedaughtermedia.com